Teen ELI Readers B1

The ELI Readers collection is a complete range of books and plays for readers of all ages, ranging from captivating contemporary stories to timeless classics. There are three series, each catering for a different age group; Young ELI Readers, Teen ELI Readers and Young Adult ELI Readers. The books are carefully edited and beautifully illustrated to capture the essence of the stories and plots. The readers are supplemented with 'Focus on' texts packed with background cultural information about the writers and their lives and times.

Mary Flagan

Val's Diary

Illustrated by Laura Ferracioli

Teen ELI Readers

Val's Diary
by Mary Flagan
Activities by Manuela De Angelis
Illustrated by Laura Ferracioli

ELI Readers
Founder and Series Editors
Paola Accattoli, Grazia Ancillani, Daniele Garbuglia (Art Director)

Eli Editorial Staff
Natalie Bayne

Eli Design Department
Fabrizio Redaelli

Production Manager
Francesco Capitano

Photo credits
Shutterstock

The publisher would like to take this opportunity to thank Sarah Howell for her contribution to the development of the project

The publisher would like to take this opportunity to thank Lisa Kester Dodgson

P.O. Box 6
62019 Recanati MC
Italy
T +39 071750701
F +39 071977851
info@elionline.com
www.elionline.com

Typeset in 13 / 18 pt Monotype Dante

Printed in Italy by Tecnostampa Recanati - ERT301.01
ISBN 978-88-536-0502-3

First edition: September 2009

www.elireaders.com

Contents

6	Characters	
8	Before you read	
10	Chapter 1	**Summer in the Country**
18	Activities	
20	Chapter 2	**A Surprise Meeting**
28	Activities	
30	Chapter 3	**Who's a Good Cook?**
38	Activities	
40	Chapter 4	**Val's First Date**
48	Activities	
50	Chapter 5	**All's Well that Ends Well**
56	Activities	
58	Focus on...	**A World of Cakes**
60	Focus on...	**Dear Diary...**
62	Test yourself	
63	Syllabus	

These icons indicate the parts of the story that are recorded

start ▶ **stop** ■

Characters

Mrs Smollett
John Crane
Mark
Doctor Smollett
Sally

Before you read

Vocabulary

1 Label the picture with the words.

lake wood
bike track
manor house

Vocabulary

2 Unscramble the letters in the silly words to find out what Val's dad and Jason are saying.

I'm Mr Rowell. My dream is to live in the ceyorsnidut. *countryside*

3 Hi! My name's Jason and I can't wait to go to the country to our lettil cottage. ....

1 In the country the air is canle and the people are hdrawkoirng!
....
....

2 I'll do some vegetable gardening: I'll grow and eat our own crortas, tmoateos, lttueec, oonins and patsotoe.
....
....
....
....
....

4 Wow! I can make a teer hsoue and use my rkcuscka!
....
....

5 Let's go simwmngi and hiking ! Come on !
....

Vocabulary

3 Match the words to make phrases.

	g Polluted	a restaurant
1	Block of	b on the phone
2	Shopping	c mall
3	Fast food	d flats
4	Best	e friend
5	Chat	f games
6	Computer	g air

Grammar

4 Guess what Val is saying and complete the text.

I love living in ...*the*... city! My little flat is so beautiful and (1) .... I look out from the window I (2) .... see all these cars on the streets. It's always so (3) .... with people. Let's go to the cinema and then have a burger at the fast food restaurant! How (4) .... spending hours on the phone, chatting with your best friend? I couldn't do (5) .... it!

Vocabulary

5 Complete the spider web with the adjectives. Then add your own.

relaxing	boring	quiet
busy	noisy	clean
exciting	polluted	

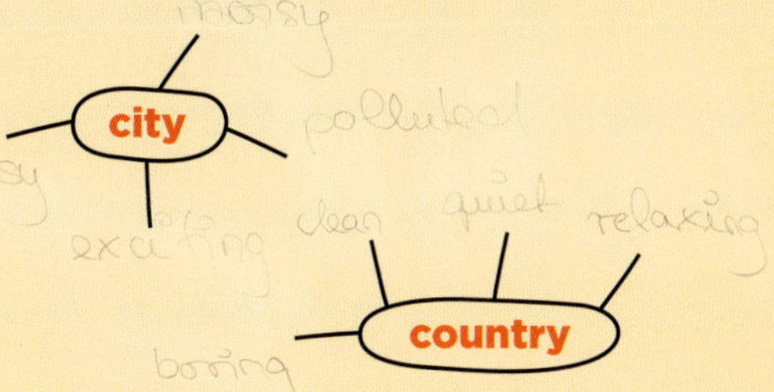

Speaking

6 Over to you now! Which do you prefer? Life in the city or life in the countryside? Why? You might change your mind!

Chapter 1

Summer in the Country

Friday, July 1st

2 Dear Diary,

It was my birthday last Saturday.

What a disaster! I wanted a pair of rollerblades.

And what did I get? A pair of hiking boots! Yuk!

I hate the countryside. Mum was looking at me when I opened the present.

'Oh, Val, you're never happy!' she said.

Well, I wanted rollerblades not hiking boots, but I didn't say it.

And I couldn't have a birthday party because school is over for the summer and all my friends are at the seaside or abroad*.

Even Sally, my best friend, is away and here I'm all alone with just my parents and my horrible little brother.

His name is Jason and he's 12, two years younger than me. I can't* stand him. He's so annoying*!

abroad in another country
can't stand don't like (strong)
(He's so) annoying (he) makes me angry

He gave me this diary for my birthday.

What a stupid present!

I'm only writing in it because I'm so bored. It's going to be an awful* summer.

awful very bad

Saturday, July 2nd

Dear Diary,

We're going on holiday to Greenhill tomorrow. Dad's driving. It's a small village in the middle of nowhere about 20 miles from the city centre. Mum and Dad want to go and live there forever. They say that they're tired of all the traffic and air* pollution here.

Jason is really happy. His rucksack is packed and ready.

He put in nails, a hammer, a little saw, a rope, a blanket, a water bottle, a magnifying glass, a box of matches and even three tins of meat! He calls me Friday and I'm fed* up with it.

I don't like playing silly* games like Robinson Crusoe! Nobody asked me for my opinion.

air pollution dangerous and damaging gases and chemicals in the air
fed up with tired of
silly stupid

I like living here in the city. I've got my school and all my friends and my bedroom here in our little flat*. I certainly don't want to go and live in Greenhill! What a silly name for a town anyway!

'We'll just have a nice relaxing holiday there and then we'll decide,' said Mum. Hmph! What she really means is that she'll decide! Democracy doesn't exist in this family!

flat: apartment

Sunday, July 3rd

Dear Diary,

We arrived at Greenhill today. It's a tiny* village. There isn't even a cinema or a fast food restaurant!

There are only about ten houses, a church and a kind of corner shop which sells everything under the sun: food, newspapers, clothes and even shoes. There's a kind of bar at the back where you can eat and drink. There are only about three tables.

My brother is over the moon because there's a lake, a wood and a bike* track. As soon as we arrived he ran out into the garden.

He began jumping about and shouting*.

'Mum, Dad, look!'

Mum, Dad and I ran into the garden.

'What is it?' asked Dad.

'A tree that's just perfect to make a treehouse,' Jason said.

tiny very small
bike track bicycle path
shouting saying in a loud voice

'That's a really good idea! I'll help you,' said Dad, 'I'll be Robinson and you can be Friday.'

'No', said Jason, 'you can be Robinson, I'll be your son and Val can be Fri...'

'Don't even think about it,' I said. 'Now I'm going into the house to find my bedroom and I don't want to be disturbed for the rest of the holiday. I certainly will not be Friday.' I put up a DO NOT DISTURB sign on my bedroom door. But I know that Jason is going to drive me crazy anyway.

Oh, when can I go home?

After-reading Activities

Reading

1 **Val and her family are spending a holiday in the countryside but not everybody is happy about it! Tick the happy ones.**

- **A** Mr Rowell ☒
- **B** Mrs Rowell ☒
- **C** Val ☐
- **D** Jason ☒

2 **Decide if the statements are true (T) or false (F). Correct the false sentences.**

		T	F
	Val has recently had a birthday.	☑	☐
1	Val is fed up with living in the city.	☐	☒
2	Jason's rucksack is empty.	☐	☒
3	Jason is going to make a treehouse.	☒	☐
4	The sign on Val's bedroom door says: You are welcome! Do not distub	☐	☒
5	Greenhill is a big town. Greenhill is a tiny village.	☐	☒

3 **Collect information about Greenhill village from Val's diary and write notes in the table.**

Village	ten houses, a church
Facilities - shops, etc	corner shop, a bus
Nature	a lake, a wood, a bike track

Grammar

4 **Complete the sentences with the verbs in the correct tense.**

want	give	shout	put up	run	put	get

Jason ....*gave*..... Val a diary for her birthday.

1 Jason .... lots of things in his rucksack.

2 Val .... rollerblades but she .... hiking boots.

3 Jason ran in the garden and ....

4 Val .... into her bedroom.

5 Then she .... a do not disturb sign.

Vocabulary

5 **Match the phrases to their meanings.**

[*f*] democracy doesn't exist in this family

1 [ ] over the moon

2 [ ] fed up with

3 [ ] drive me crazy

4 [ ] can't stand him

5 [ ] everything under the sun

a he makes me angry

b very happy and enthusiastic

c is very annoying

d everything you can think of

e tired of something or someone

f not everyone has an equal voice in the family

Before-reading Activities

PET-Speaking

6a **Work in pairs. Each of you is going to talk on your own for about a minute.**

Student A turn to page 17.

Look at the picture. Tell your partner what you can see.

Student B turn to page 27.

Look at the picture. Tell your partner what you can see.

6b **What do you think is going to happen in the next chapter?**

Chapter 2

A Surprise Meeting

Monday, July 4th

3 Dear Diary,

I have to admit that this little house in Greenhill is quite nice. It's yellow and there's a small porch* above the front door. There's a little garden all around the house. It's pretty but there isn't a telephone. I lost* my temper when I discovered this. 'How can I survive without a telephone?' I shouted, red as a beetroot*. (I always go red when I get angry!) Dad burst* out laughing and Mum said that I could do my holiday homework without any interruptions. Oh, yeah!

There's a little vegetable garden behind the house and Dad is going to buy lots of tools* and things so that he can do some gardening. He wants to plant carrots, onions, potatoes, tomatoes and lettuce and says that we'll only eat our own vegetables from now on.

porch roof over the entrance of a house
lost my temper got angry
beetroot a dark red vegetable
burst out laughing laughed suddenly and strongly
tools equipment to use (here) in the garden

I'm worried that this means we really will move to Greenhill forever. 'Ah! This is the life', says Dad, 'clean air ... contact with nature ... good, honest, hardworking people ... .'

I should probably mention* that Dad also has a little garden at home. He has strawberry plants and one tomato plant. Every year in spring he says: 'Ah! This year we can pick some lovely strawberries' or 'we'll have our own tomatoes to eat.' But nothing ever grows and Dad is always really disappointed. He blames the air pollution.

Dad's happy here in the country. I don't understand it at all. I think it's boring. There's nothing to do and nobody to talk to.

Dad's crazy! And, the neighbours* are very silly, too! As soon as we arrived they all suddenly appeared with fruit, vegetables, cakes and one of them even brought a hen! My brother says that he wants to keep it as a pet. He called it Polly. What an idiot!

mention say
neighbours people living next to our house

Tuesday, July 5th

Dear Diary,

Mrs Perry our neighbour is unbearable*. She comes to our house all the time. This morning the doorbell rang at half past seven. Of course we were all asleep and it gave us a terrible fright*. Dad ran down to open the door in his pyjamas. I think maybe he also fell down the stairs because I heard a loud bang but when he opened the door all he said was, 'Oh hello, Mrs Perry ... for us ... really? ... very kind of you ... come in. Would you like a cup of tea?'

She brought a chocolate cake for us. I must admit it was gorgeous and she actually made it herself. Ten minutes later we were all in the garden having breakfast. When Mrs Perry saw me in my pyjamas she said, 'Poor little girl ... so pale* and thin. Our wonderful healthy air here at Greenhill will soon give you lovely rosy* cheeks.' Who does she think she is? Pale and thin indeed! I certainly don't want rosy cheeks. I'm fine just the way I am!

unbearable horrible
fright shock
pale white
rosy pink

Wednesday, July 6th

Dear Diary,

I found a letter in the post box this morning. It was addressed to us.

The Rowell Family
Buttercup House
Greenhill

Of course I opened it immediately. Well I'm part of the Rowell family, after all! It was an invitation.

On behalf of the residents of Greenhill, I'm pleased to invite Mr and Mrs Rowell and their children Val and Jason to our annual fair at the Happy Village Club.*

After the prestigious darts* competition there will be games, dancing and refreshments* for everyone.*

Looking forward to meeting you,
John Crane, Mayor

P.S. If you want to take part in the competition ask for details at the Happy Village Club, Greenhill.*

fair town party or festival
prestigious important
darts game with small arrows
refreshments food and drinks
take part compete

Val's Diary

Dad drove into town at once to put* his name down and so tonight we're all going to the fair. The Happy Village Club is located near the corner shop which I mentioned earlier.

Eleven people are taking part in the competition. That's probably all of Greenhill's adult population! Dad is sure he's going to win. He always thinks he's going to win. But he never does! I don't* mind going. At least there'll be a telephone there and I can call Sally. She's my best friend.

I really miss her.

put (his name) down enter
don't mind do not like or do not hate (neutral)

Thursday, July 7th

Dear Diary,

Last night we went to the fair. I couldn't speak to Sally because she was out with her brother.

What a pity!

Dad came second!

Doctor Smollett, the town doctor, won the competition. His wife and their two children were there too. Mark is 12 years old like Jason and Luke is 16.

He's gorgeous*!

My brother played cards all night with Mark and left me alone. Luke's got brown hair and green eyes. He's much taller than me.

When I first saw him I'm sure I went as red as a beetroot! Then Dad introduced us.

'And this is my little girl, Val'.

gorgeous (here) good-looking

I felt so humiliated* and angry I'm sure my face was every colour under the sun. Luke probably thought I was some sort of extraterrestrial*.

It's all my father's fault*. Calling me a little girl! In front of the most handsome boy in the whole world.

What a disaster! I feel so humiliated.

Mum made friends with Luke's mother.

Her name's Sarah. She invited us to their house for dinner one night soon.

Wow! I can't wait!

humiliated ashamed and insulted
extraterrestrial alien
fault (here) blame

After-reading Activities

Reading

1 Reorder these events in Val's life in the correct chronological order. The first sentence is already given.

A The Rowells were invited to the Greenhill annual fair. 4

B Val did not like her because she said Val was so pale and thin. 3

C Mr Rowell took part in the darts competition. 5

D Val liked Luke very much and went red when she saw him. 6

E Mrs Perry brought a chocolate cake at seven o'clock. 2

F Neighbours brought them fruit, cakes and a hen. 1

G The Rowell family were invited to the Smollett's house. 7

2 Complete the table with information about Doctor Smollet's family.

2 children

Doctor Smollett	the [illegible] doctor, won the competition
His wife	Sarah Smollett, 2 children
Mark	17 years
Luke	16 years, brown hair, green eyes, taller; he's gorgeous, handsome boy than Val

Grammar

3 What are the characters going to do? Make sentences with the prompts.

Mr Rowell / grow / vegetables

Mr Rowell is going to grow vegetables.

1 The Rowell family / go / to the fair

2 Val / not survive / without a telephone

3 Jason / keep / hen / pet

4 Val / meet / Luke again

5 The Rowells / have dinner / Smollett family

Vocabulary

4 Use the definitions to complete the puzzle and find out how Val felt.

Another word for beautiful.

1 Opposite of happy.

2 Red juicy vegetables.

3 A vegetable that can make you cry.

4 Rosy cheeks mean that you are...

5 A letter which invites you somewhere.

6 You wear them when you sleep.

7 Somebody from another planet.

8 Val went red as a...

9 A game with little arrows and a target.

H U M I L I A T E D

PET-Writing

5 You are Val. You are planning to give a party for your birthday. Write an invitation to your friends. In this invitation you should

- say what day is the party
- say at what time is the party
- say where you will give the party

Write **35-45 words.**

Chapter 3

Who's a Good Cook?

Friday, July 8th

4 Dear Diary,

Dad went out this morning to buy a newspaper and he met Doctor Smollett!

He set* a date for the dinner at his house!

'We'll expect* you then on Monday night at about 7 o'clock, if you're free, of course,' said Doctor Smollett.

'We'll be delighted to come. If my wife has time, she'll make a cake. She makes delicious cakes. She and Val win cooking contests all the time,' said Dad. Of course he was lying*!

When Dad told us the good news I was so happy that I couldn't believe it.

'That's wonderful,' said my mother, 'I'll take one of my super salads.'

'No, dear, we're taking a cake,' said Dad.

set a date decided on a day
expect wait for
lying not telling the truth

'A cake,' shouted my mother. 'Where are we going to get a cake? There isn't a good cake shop in Greenhill!'

'You're going to make it, my dear,' said Dad.

'Me? I don't know how to make cakes. No, my dear, tomorrow you are going to buy a cake!'

'That's impossible!'

'Why?'

'Because I told them that you're a terrific cook. If we take a shop cake, they'll know I was lying!'

Mum got all red in the face and I decided it was time to make* myself scarce! It's better to take cover when Mum gets angry!

make myself scarce leave quickly

Saturday, July 9th

Dear diary

Help! I'm desperate!

This morning Dad and I went on a VIM (Very Important Mission). If we don't find a cake for Monday evening Mum says we're not going to dinner! I suggested going to the shop in Greenhill but Dad decided to ask our friendly neighbour, Mrs Perry.

Dad explained our problem and she accepted with great joy.

'Well, of course I'll do it,' she said, 'and Val will help me. Won't you, Val? Do you like baking?'

'No, not at all,' I wanted to shout, but Dad winked* at me and so I said, 'Of course, Mrs Perry, I'd love to help you.'

'Aren't you a lovely little girl,' she said smiling, 'I'll just go and get my recipe book.'

Mrs Perry went into the kitchen and came back with a big red box. She took off the lid* and turned it upside* down. A mountain of papers fell out.

winked closed one eye quickly then opened it
lid (here) top of a box
upside down with the top where the bottom usually is

There was a recipe on each piece of paper. What an odd* recipe book!

'What's your favourite cake, Val?' she asked.

I didn't know what to say but Dad came to my rescue 'Fruit flan. Val loves fruit flan.' (I can't stand fruit flan!)

'But that's really simple to make,' said Mrs Perry.

'I love it. It tastes so good!' I said.

'Well alright then,' she said, 'let's look for a recipe for fruit flan. I don't really need a recipe but I forget everything all the time.'

When she eventually found the recipe Dad put it in his pocket and said 'We'll bring you all the ingredients tomorrow morning. Val loves shopping.'

I don't love shopping at all but I don't think I have any choice!

odd strange

Sunday, July 10th

Dear Diary,

Dad woke me up at 7 o'clock this morning! 7 o'clock! I can't even sleep during the holidays in this family! He sent me to buy all the ingredients for the cake. (The grocery shop in Greenhill is open 7 days a week.) ['grəʊsərɪ] Subst. = Lebensmittelgeschäft

Ingredients for topping

1 litre of custard
apricots
1 bunch each of green and black grapes
strawberries
raspberries
1 packet of jelly
whipping cream

Method

In a bowl* mix the flour, sugar and walnuts together. Then add the butter, egg yolks and milk and beat well. Put the mixture into a well-greased cake tin and bake for 20 minutes. Allow* to cool. Decorate with the custard and the fruit cut into pieces. Cover with the jelly. Put into the fridge for at least 2 hours. Serve with the whipped cream.

bowl deep plate
allow permit

The shop was full of people and while I was waiting I picked up a cream* bun and started to eat it. Then I heard a voice say behind me:

'Hi, Val!' I turned around. It was Luke!

'Oh! Hi!' He was smiling at me.

'You're coming tomorrow night, aren't you?'

'Mmmm ... yeah*,' I said with my mouth full.

He burst out laughing and said, 'You've got cream on your nose,' and took out a tissue* and rubbed* it off.

I was so embarrassed!

Oh, why did I eat that cream bun?

cream bun small cream cake
yeah yes (colloquial)
tissue paper cloth
rubbed (it) off cleaned (it)

After-reading Activities

Reading

1 Complete the sentences.

Dad went out to the shop and ......*met Doctor Smollett*......

1 Mr Rowell lied to Doctor Smollett. He said that ....
2 Val and her dad asked Mrs Perry if ....
3 Mrs Perry decided to ....
4 Val met Luke at the shop. He asked her if ....
5 Luke laughed because ....

2 Complete the table about Val with information so far.

	Food	Habits	People
Likes	cream bun		Luke
Dislikes	fruit flan	to get up early	Mrs Perry

Grammar

3 Complete the following if-sentences.

Doctor Smollett asks the family to come *if they have time*

1 If Val's mother has time, she ....
2 If they take a shop cake, the Smolletts ....
3 When Mrs Rowell gets angry, everybody ....
4 They won't go to the dinner, if they ....

Vocabulary

4 Choose the correct alternative.

The invitation to the Smollett's house is for *lunchtime* / *evening*.

1 Val *was* / *wasn't* happy to help Mrs Perry.
2 Mrs Perry keeps a big recipe *book* / *box*.
3 A fruit flan is *easy* / *difficult* to make.
4 You *need* / *don't need* an oven to make the fruit flan.
5 Val met Luke *inside* / *outside* the grocery shop.

Vocabulary

5 Match the recipe vocabulary to their definitions.

	d	ingredients	**a**	a group of fruit growing on a single stem
1	c	yolk	**b**	a measurement
2	f	base	**c**	the yellow part of an egg
3	e	topping	**d**	food you need for a recipe
4	b	g	**e**	the top part of a cake
5	a	bunch	**f**	the bottom part of a cake

PET-Writing

6 The Rowells have recently moved into the house next to you and you would like to introduce yourself to them. Write a note to the family. In your note you should

- Introduce yourself
- Give them a piece of useful information about the neighbourhood
- Offer to do something for the family

Write **35-45 words**.

Before-reading Activities

Speaking and Listening

7 Tick (✓) the things you think will happen.

A Val's Dad goes looking at houses. ☑
B The Rowell family go for tea at the manor. ☐
C Val and Luke go swimming. ☑
D Val kisses Luke. ☐

▶ 5 **8 Val is very anxious about the dinner. Will the Smolletts find out that neither Val nor her mother are terrific cooks? Listen to the next chapter.**

Chapter 4

Val's First Date

Monday, July 11th

5 Dear Diary,

I don't believe this! Dad got me up again at 7 o'clock! Is there no peace at all in the country?

'Mrs Perry is waiting for you,' he said, 'people get up early here.'

'That's just why I want to go back to our beautiful flat as soon as possible,' I said.

'Come on. The* early bird catches the worm. And Val, be nice, hmm? She's a sweet old lady.'

When I arrived at Mrs Perry's house, the cake was ready. I think people in the country don't go to sleep at all!

She asked me to follow her into the kitchen. There were two cakes on the table - a big one and a little one.

'Two,' I exclaimed*.

'Yes! I made one for you for breakfast. You can tell me if it's good or not!'

the early bird catches the worm (proverb) being early will give you advantage
exclaimed said in a surprised voice

Evening

Dear Diary,

I'm so happy I can't wait until tomorrow to write about what happened at the Smollett's house. Mrs Perry's fruit flan was a big success. Everyone said that it was delicious. And that Mum was a great cook.

She was very embarrassed!

Poor Dad. If* looks could kill!

Luke's brother, Mark, is sick so Jason didn't leave us alone the whole evening! What a horrible brother I've got. But never* mind that. Here's the news - when I got back I found this note in my pocket:

*My friends and I are going swimming
in the lake the day after tomorrow.
Why don't you come with us?
I'll meet you at the Happy Village Club
at 4 o'clock.
Please come!*

Luke

Wow! A date*!

This is my first date. Maybe next year my diary will be full of photos and secret letters like all my friends. Please come, Luke. Oh, I'm so excited. I can't wait to phone Sally and tell her everything. Wednesday is so far* away!

if looks could kill Mrs Rowell looks at her husband in an angry way
never mind (that) it doesn't matter
date romantic appointment
far away distant

Tuesday, July 12th

Dear Diary,

An invitation came in the post this morning from Lord Greenhill. It was an invitation to tea at his manor* tomorrow afternoon. Mum is so excited; it is ridiculous*! I have absolutely no intention of going! I don't want to meet a silly old lord and besides, tomorrow afternoon I'm going swimming with Luke. But I won't tell Mum that just yet.

Dad and I went to look at some houses today. I do not want to live here forever even if Luke is really good-looking!

I'll lose all my friends.

Luckily one house was too small and another wasn't big enough, one had no garden or else it was too big.

Dad didn't find anything that he liked.

I'm keeping* my fingers crossed!

manor very large and elegant house
ridiculous very silly
keeping my fingers crossed an action which brings good luck

Wednesday, July 13th
Early afternoon

Dear Diary,

Yippee*! I'm all alone. They're all at tea at the manor.

Mum was acting really crazy this morning; she asked Dad to take her to our flat. She wanted to get some smart* clothes to wear to meet Lord Greenhill. Mum wore the same dress that she bought for my aunt's wedding and my brother wore a jacket and a dickey-bow*. He looked ridiculous! He even had gel in his hair! At twelve! Mum was mad at me because I told her that I wasn't going!

It's nearly time to meet Luke. Oh, I'm so nervous. Still can't decide what to wear.

yippee That's wonderful! (exclamation)
smart formal / elegant
dickey-bow bow tie , boy / man's clothing worn around the neck

Evening

Dear Diary,

Luke and I went to the lake with his friends. While we were swimming underwater he kissed me! Yes! HE KISSED ME!

I got a terrible fright. I swallowed* about a ton of water and nearly drowned*! I didn't know what to say after that so we didn't talk on the way home. When he was going he asked:

'Can we meet tomorrow?'

'I don't know if I'm free,' I said.

'What about the day after tomorrow?'

'I don't know ... call me!'

'Ok. Bye Val.'

I'm a total idiot! A gorgeous boy asks me for a date and I tell him: 'I don't know, call me!'

How can he call me if we don't have a telephone?

swallowed put into your mouth, into your stomach
drowned died underwater

Maybe Dad is right. I really am a baby sometimes!

Mum, Dad and Jason came back from the manor. They are still acting really strangely. But what's new? They always act really strangely! I've got so much to think about. Oh, where's Sally? Just when I need her!

After-reading Activities

PET-Reading

1 Read the summary and choose the correct word for each space. For each question choose A, B, C or D.

Example:

0 **A** have **B** having **C** had **D** is

Answer:		A	B	C	D
	0	▭	▭	▬ (filled)	▭

The following morning, Mrs Perry (0)......*had*...... made delicious fruit flans ready, one for the dinner and a (1).............. one just for Val's breakfast. The evening (2).............. the Smolletts' was a (3).............. What's more, when Val got back, she found a note in her (4).............. It was Luke's, asking her to go (5).............. in the lake on Wednesday. That was Val's first date! (6).............. the day after, another invitation came from Lord Greenhill for the afternoon which she was supposed to go swimming with Luke! In the meantime Mr and Mrs Rowell were looking (7).............. a house to buy in the village. Val was a little worried about it. At last all the family went to tea at the manor, but Val managed to stay home, even though her mum was (8).............. at her. She is looking forward to meeting Luke, but she doesn't know what to (9).............. !

1	**A** small	**B** smallest	**C** smaller	**D** bigger
2	**A** in	**B** at	**C** on	**D** into
3	**A** disaster	**B** wonderful	**C** mess	**D** success
4	**A** pocket	**B** handbag	**C** rucksack	**D** car
5	**A** swim	**B** swam	**C** swimming	**D** swum
6	**A** So	**B** And	**C** Although	**D** But
7	**A** for	**B** at	**C** with	**D** after
8	**A** crazy	**B** happy	**C** mad	**D** glad
9	**A** say	**B** wear	**C** sing	**D** read

Grammar

2 Complete the sentences with the right form of the simple past or past continuous.

When Luke ....*arrived*.... (arrive) at the shop, Val *was eating* (eat) a cream bun.

1 While Val ...slept........ (sleep), Mrs Perry was baking (bake) the cakes.

2 While the two families .... (eat) dinner, Mark .... (be) sick in bed.

3 Mr Rowell .... (like) the houses he .... (see).

4 While they .... (swim), Luke .... (kiss) Val.

5 When Luke .... (go) he .... (ask) to see her again.

3 The right clothes for the right occasion! Look at these outfits and decide where or when to wear them. Discuss in pairs.

1 long black dress with pearl necklace and high heeled shoes for women.

2 jeans, t-shirt and trainers.

3 black jacket and trousers with bow tie and smart shoes for men.

4 grey suit, white shirt and tie for men.

5 shorts, top and slippers.

Before-reading Activity

Speaking

4 Tick (✓) what you think will happen. Then listen and check.

1 Val doesn't think about Luke. ☐

2 Val speaks to Sally for advice. ☐

3 The Rowells find the house of their dreams. ☐

4 Val decides to become a policewoman. ☐

5 Val leaves Greenhill. ☐

Chapter 5

All's Well that Ends Well

Thursday, July 14th

5 pm

6 Dear Diary,

I don't know what is happening to me. My life is turning upside-down*. Yesterday a boy kissed me for the first time in my life and today my parents said, 'Val, Jason, come and see the house of our dreams.'

Here! In Greenhill!

This afternoon we all went to look at the house of their dreams. It's right* opposite the bus stop for the city so I suppose that is a positive aspect, but I still prefer our old flat.

I went to the bar in the centre of town and called Sally.

Misery! She's still away. Just when I need her. When I think about Sally I feel really miserable. I don't want to lose her. She's my best friend. Eight years of school together, sitting at the same desk and now...

upside-down (here) changing
right (here) directly

Sally says that I'm lucky going to live in the country because I can keep all the animals I want. I never said I wanted to be a vet*! I want to be a fashion designer. Sally really wants to be a policewoman or a detective. (Only because she once solved a puzzle that she found in an old Egyptian souvenir.)

I know she'll change* her mind.

vet veterinary surgeon (doctor for animals)
change her mind make a new decision

Thursday, July 14th
10 pm

Dear Diary,

What's* going on? Mum and Dad disappeared again at about 6 o'clock. They returned almost at once and Mum started to pack immediately. Dad said 'It's time to leave kids. We're going back to our flat in the city.'

'Why?' I asked.

'Your mother and I have a* million things to do now that we're going to move house. In one month we're going to come here to settle* down forever.'

'I'm not!' I shouted.

'Not what? Returning to our flat in the city or coming back here to Greenhill?'

I didn't know what to say. I don't know what to say now.

I feel confused!! I don't want to go back to the city just yet. What about Luke?

what's going on? what's happening?
a million (things to do) lots of (things to do)
settle down live in a new house forever

But I don't want to leave Sally and all my friends either.

Mum says that I never know what I want. Dad says that this is normal when you're 14.

I think they're also a bit confused! Anyway before we left I wrote a note to Luke with my address and telephone number.

I hope he calls me and if he doesn't ... I'll call him.

Whew! What a holiday. I've got so much to tell Sally!

After-reading Activities

Reading

1 Write the questions for these answers.

Why does Val feel like an idiot?
Because she told him to call her and she doesn't have a phone .

1 .... ?
Luke kissed Val and she nearly drowned.

2 .... ?
In Greenhill, opposite the bus stop for the city.

3 .... ?
She wants to become a fashion designer.

4 .... ?
They were leaving because they had many things to do.

5 .... ?
She felt miserable and also confused.

2 Val's mood changes a lot. Say how she felt when...

Val had to go on holiday in Greenhill.	*angry*
1 Val arrived in Greenhill.	....
2 Her father introduced her as his little girl.	....
3 Val bumped into him at the grocery shop.	....
4 Val received a note from Luke.	....
5 Her parents looked at a house to buy.	....

Grammar

3 Match the two halves of the sentences.

so that   although   while   so   because   ~~and~~

I hope he calls me ....*and*........ if he doesn't I'll call him.

1 Mr and Mrs Rowell have found a dream home .... they are going to move soon.

2 Val wants to be a fashion designer .... Sally would like to be a detective.

3 Val did not like living in Greenhill .... she doesn't want to leave now.

4 Val feels miserable .... she doesn't want to lose Sally.

5 Val sends a note to Luke .... he can call her.

PET-Grammar

4 Here are some sentences about the story.
For each question, complete the second sentence so that it means the same as the first.
Use no more than three words.
Write only the missing words.

Example

0 Most people still prefer personal shopping to shopping on the Internet.
For most people shopping on the Internet is not .... personal shopping.

Answer:

0	as popular as

1 Val would like to go back to the city instead of staying in Greenhill.
Val .... back to the city than stay in Greenhill.

2 Mrs Rowell is not able to cook a good cake.
Mrs Rowell .... a good cake.

3 It is likely that Luke will call Val when she is in the city.
Luke .... Val when she is in the city.

4 If Val goes to live in Greenhill, she will date Luke.
Val will not date Luke .... she goes to live in Greenhill.

5 It's a good idea for us to live in the country.
We .... in the country.

Writing

5 **Write a letter from Val to Sally telling her all about this surprising holiday. Start like this:**
Dear Sally,
You could never believe what happened to me in Greenhill!

A World of Cakes

Pastry shops, bakeries, cake shops are everybody's favourite places to stop and snoop around. Trouble is that all those gorgeous cakes are rarely labelled and we are forced to resort to the pointing and the 'One of those, please!' This alphabetical list will help you out!

Bath Buns

They were invented by Dr W. Oliver, an 18th Century physician, who treated visitors to the famous Bath Spa. His bun proved so popular, and his patients grew so fat, that he had to invent a plain biscuit - the Bath Oliver biscuit - for his patients to eat instead. The chunks of sugar sprinkled on the top of this otherwise rather plain bun were originally sugar-coated caraway seeds.

Bread 'n' Butter Pudding

In the past it was a way for poor people to use up leftover stale bread. It is actually made from slices of bread soaked in milk, with sugar, raisins and spices (cinnamon and nutmeg). It is traditionally eaten hot with custard.

Belgian Buns

There are several cakes (and biscuits) named after places, and the question is whether this name actually reflects their place of origin. As a matter of fact, it seems that no Italian have ever eaten or heard of a Florentine in Florence, and that the best Chelsea buns seem to be baked in Cambridge, and that Danish pastries do not bear any resemblance to pastries made in Denmark. So nobody can confirm that Belgian Buns - an iced bun with a cherry garnish - come from Belgium.

Chelsea Buns

Was this cake called after the place of its origin? Actually, the existence in London of a place called The Chelsea Bun House in Grosvenor Row, Pimlico, but not exactly Chelsea, is proved by an old print at the British Museum. It also seems that Jonathan Swift visited it in 1711 and got a stale bun for a penny. The place was even patronised by George II and Queen Charlotte. Charles Dickens also mentions it in Barnaby Rudge (the beginning of chapter 42) and in Bleak House (chapter 53). This delicious cake is curiously square but made of a spiral of a raisin-spotted dough. It can be enjoyed in the traditional biting way, or by unrolling the spiral and nibbling as you go.

Doughnuts

Another cake derived from the problem of leftovers, as the first doughnuts were reportedly made to use up leftover bits of bread dough. The basic doughnut is a ball of dough, covered in sugar, with jam in the centre or a ring of dough covered in sugar. From the USA comes the habit for any kind of toppings, some involve cinnamon and chocolate. It has been made famous all over the world by Homer Simpson.

Muffins

Here's another big transatlantic favourite. Traditionally, it is a soft white-bread cake, split and toasted with jam on. Nowadays globalised muffins have become home-bakeable cakes from a bag of already prepared self-raising flour to be bought at any supermarket.

Dear Diary...

'I never travel without my diary - one should always have something sensational to read in the train.'

Gwendolen Fairfax from *The Importance of Being Ernest* by Oscar Wilde.

Diaries, Journals, Logs, Weblogs, however we call them, they may be like an addictive habit which one can't do without, or a purge to get something off the chest, a pain or a guilt. Others seem like an affirmation of the writers' existence, as if by writing it down, it has actually happened. Diaries are usually thought to be a cathartic experience for writers who express their emotions and detail their responses to events. Writing a diary represents an effort to process experience, to order it and make sense of it. Psychologists have often pointed out how writing a diary can have a positive impact on health. And then there are the online diaries - personal weblogs. Here the motives are different, because they are intended to be public and therefore probably lack candour. Most bloggers will be thinking 'My mum could read this.'

Throughout history, diaries have given an interesting insight into the past. Not only have they recorded the life of the writers but also the events of a country. Several diaries have hit a historical status and have remained as best sellers on literary lists throughout the world like for example Samuel Pepys' Journals, Lewis Carroll's and Virginia Woolf's.

Samuel Pepys (1633-1703) is the earliest diarist who is well known today; his diaries, now in Magdalene College, Cambridge, were first transcribed and published in 1825. Pepys first managed to make his journal not only a record of business transaction but also the chronicle of personal events.

Lewis Carroll (pen name for Charles Lutwidge Dodgson) the inventive writer of *Alice in Wonderland* and *Through the Looking Glass* had kept a diary nearly all his life (13 plus other 4 missing volumes). They throw a light on Victorian life and mentality, and on his peculiar attitude on word play, logic and fantasy.

Virginia Woolf, the well-known British writer of *Mrs Dalloway, To the Lighthouse* and *The Waves* began keeping a quite emotional diary around the age of 15, in 1897. Her diaries provide us with a view of her thought processes. The reader can see how she feels and how she develops the characters of her novels. Since her later life was influenced by a severe depression that lead her to suicide, her diary can also give great insight into how depression can affect life.

Fictional diaries are also both entertaining and informative. The most popular of them have recently been:

Adrian Albert Mole (born April 2, 1967) is the fictional protagonist in a series of books by English author Sue Townsend from 1982 onwards. In her six books about Adrian, she pictured the inner life of an adolescent boy in a realistic and humorous way. They also give a touch of Britain from the Thatcher period to the most contemporary New Labour days - dysfunctional families, working-class drinking, unemployment, feminism, racism and Iraq War.

Bridget Jones is the 30-something heroine created by Helen Fielding in *Bridget Jones's Diary* published in 1997. It brilliantly evokes the life of a single girl in the late '90s with all her worries about weight and diet, love problems, emotional ups and downs, humorously witty.

Test Yourself

1 Decide if the sentences are true (T) or false (F).

		T	F
	The Rowells have gone on holiday to the seaside.	☐	☑
1	Greenhill is a little village in the countryside.	☐	☐
2	There is no telephone at home.	☐	☐
3	Mrs Perry cooks delicious cakes.	☐	☐
4	The Rowells make friends with the Smolletts.	☐	☐
5	Luke is not very good-looking.	☐	☐
6	Val has a date with Jason.	☐	☐
7	Luke kisses Val underwater.	☐	☐
8	The Rowells are going to buy a house in Greenhill.	☐	☐
9	Val is happy to go back home.	☐	☐

2 TRIVIA QUIZ. How much do you remember of Val's story? Answer the questions.

Who said 'Poor little girl, so pale and thin'.

Mrs Perry.

1 What's Luke's mother's name?

....

2 Where does Val's dad come in the darts competition?

....

3 Who said 'I'll take one of my super salads'.

....

4 What time does Val meet Luke to go swimming?

....

5 Who goes to the manor?

....

6 Is custard included in the list of ingredients for the fruit flan?

....

7 What was Val eating when she bumped into Luke at the shop?

....

8 How old is Luke?

....

Syllabus

Topics
Family
Friendship, love
Holidays

Notions and concepts
Feelings
Likes and dislikes
Talking about future plans
Predictions
Ability
Actions and activities
Offers
Suggestions

Other
Verbs: regular and irregular forms
Modal verbs
Adverbs
Adjectives
Prepositions
Linkers
Comparatives and superlatives
Nouns and pronouns
Determiners

Teen ELI Readers

Stage 1
Maureen Simpson, *In Search of a Missing Friend*
Charles Dickens, *Oliver Twist*

Stage 2
Maria Luisa Banfi, *A Faraway World*
Maria Luisa Banfi, *Francesca's Love*
Maria Luisa Banfi, *The Darnley Family's Long-Lost Necklace*

Stage 3
Mary Flagan, *The Egyptian Souvenir*
Mary Flagan, *Val's Diary*
Maureen Simpson, *Destination: Karminia*
Mark Twain, *The Adventures of Huckleberry Finn*